RAND

How Does Congress Approach Population and Family Planning Issues?

Results of Qualitative Interviews with Legislative Directors

Sally Patterson
David M. Adamson

Supported by the
William and Flora Hewlett Foundation
Rockefeller Foundation
United Nations Population Fund

POPULATION MATTERS

A RAND Program of Policy-Relevant Research Communication

This report presents the results of qualitative interviews with legislative directors for members of the U.S. Congress on population-related issues. The interviews were conducted in July and August of 1997. The purpose was to deepen understanding of how legislators view these issues, what their information needs on the subject are, and how information usually reaches them. The interviews explored attitudes and knowledge about issues related to population, such as foreign relations, family planning, the environment, and immigration.

The interviews were conducted for RAND's *Population Matters* project. The primary focus of this project is synthesizing and communicating the findings and implications of existing demographic research in ways that policy audiences and other interested groups will find accessible. The project grew out of the belief, held by many in both research and policy circles, that the results of demographic research are relatively inaccessible to policy audiences and therefore have less impact than they otherwise might. One of the project's challenges is to identify key policy audiences, understand how research-based demographic information might be useful to them, and devise strategies for communicating it to them effectively. One of these key audiences is the U.S. Congress. Therefore, to help us better understand which areas of demographic research to focus on and how best to convey the findings to Congress, we decided to survey congressional audiences to get a sense of their knowledge and attitudes about population issues.

These interviews helped to shape the project's first major report (*The Value of Family Planning in Developing Countries*, by Rodolfo A. Bulatao) and a related Issue Paper ("Family Planning in Developing Countries: An Unfinished Success Story," by Julie DaVanzo and David M. Adamson).

This document should be of interest to anyone concerned with congressional knowledge of and views on population-related issues. This research was conducted within RAND's Labor and Population Program. The work was supported by grants from the William and Flora Hewlett Foundation, the Rockefeller Foundation, and the United Nations Population Fund.

For further information on the *Population Matters* project, contact:

Julie DaVanzo, Director, *Population Matters*

RAND
P.O Box 2138
1700 Main St.
Santa Monica, CA 90407-2138

Julie_DaVanzo@rand.org

Or visit the project's web site at **http://www.rand.org.popmatters**

CONTENTS

TABLE

This report presents the results of qualitative interviews with a sample of legislative directors in the U.S. Senate and the House of Representatives on subjects related to population issues and policies. The interviews explored attitudes toward issues related to population, such as foreign relations, family planning, the environment, and immigration.

Opinion on this set of issues is highly polarized. Approximately 90 percent of Congress consistently votes either uniformly to support or uniformly to oppose population-related legislation. The 10 percent comprising our target sample is thus an extremely critical group because it is likely to determine passage or failure of population-related policy initiatives. It is therefore critical to understand three points about this swing-vote group:

- How they make their choices

- What their attitudes are: For example, is there truth to the commonly held assumptions that current members of Congress tend to be isolationist, desire to cut funding for foreign aid, and regard family planning and other population programs as not valuable?

- How information reaches them and how they use it. In particular, we wanted to obtain a clearer picture of whether and how they make use of research-based information on population issues.

Because we wanted to conduct in-depth interviews, we decided not to seek the direct participation of members of Congress, who were not likely to be available for the 45 to 60 minutes required. We chose instead to interview legislative directors. Legislative directors are the senior policy advisers to members of Congress and directly advise legislators on specific policy issues. Because of their close working relationships with the members of Congress who employ them, legislative directors are uniquely positioned to know and understand the views of their members of Congress on important issues. They are also expected to act as official representatives of their employers' positions, and routinely speak on behalf of their members of Congress. Throughout the interviews, respondents clarified whether they were speaking for themselves (which was rare) or for their employers.

The sample was small (19 legislative directors—three from the Senate and 16 from the House) and not random (we selected members of Congress with mixed or inconsistent voting records on the population issues). Thus, the responses by definition do not represent the distribution across all current members of Congress. However, while these data cannot be construed to represent the opinions of all of Congress or of all congressional staff, they do provide insight into the attitudes, knowledge, and behavior of the legislators whose population-related voting patterns are not entirely in favor or opposed.

The study found that, as reported by their legislative directors, the members of Congress in our sample appeared reasonably well-informed on population-related issues and generally believed that the United States had a role to play in supporting population-assistance programs around the world. There was, however, some confusion surrounding some demographic concepts, such as *population momentum*. There was also a general lack of awareness about the magnitude of U.S. levels of population assistance relative to other types of foreign aid.

Below are highlights of the legislative directors' reports of the views and knowledge of members of Congress about population issues:

- **Most respondents felt that the United States should continue to play a leading role in international issues and foreign assistance.** This finding was somewhat surprising, given the widespread perception that the Republican-majority Congresses of the 1990s are decidedly isolationist. Most of the legislative directors we interviewed reported that the members of Congress they work for believe in a strong leadership role for the United States in world affairs.

- **Several legislative directors also stressed that their members of Congress favor increased emphasis on multilateral approaches to addressing international problems.** Believing in U.S. leadership or participation in global affairs does not translate into a desire for the United States to "go it alone" or expend inordinate resources or energy on addressing population issues. Instead, the members of Congress supported multilateral approaches that are based on international cooperation and involve multinational institutions. Security issues are an exception to the support for multilateralism.

- **A majority of interviewees felt that world population growth was a problem, but not an urgent one.** There was general consensus among the interviewees that the rate of world population growth was too high. Population growth was viewed as a problem by Republicans and Democrats alike, including both supporters and opponents of funding for family planning. On the other hand, few considered world population growth to be an urgent problem.

- **Most legislative directors reported that their members of Congress felt that the United States should address population issues, but not necessarily aggressively.** The answer to whether the United States should try to address world population growth was mainly affirmative. The respondents said their members of Congress generally believed the United States should play a role in addressing population issues, but then typically qualified their support by saying the United States is already doing what it can, that the United States must be careful not to impose its values on other nations, or that there is a limit to how much the United States can be expected to fund.

- **Nearly unanimous support was expressed for U.S. support of voluntary family planning.** The legislative directors said their employers support foreign aid for voluntary family planning as an appropriate way to address growth rates in developing countries. All but one, employed by a Democratic member of Congress, supported family planning as a means of addressing this need. The stated attitudes on support for family planning assistance did not vary by party identity, length of time in office, abortion position, or the position of the member of Congress generally on population-related issues.

- **The abortion issue figures prominently in the debate on family planning.** In recent years, abortion has tended to overshadow other considerations in the congressional discussion and voting on international family planning. Those legislative directors whose employers were classified as "mostly opposed" often raised abortion as soon as family planning was mentioned in the interview, volunteering that their members of Congress want to support making contraception available but not abortion. Despite this prominent connection, however, the discussants did not demonstrate an awareness of links between the two issues outside a political context (for example, what research has shown about the relationship between abortion rates and the availability of contraception.)

- **Congress would benefit from research-based information on a variety of population-related topics addressing specific, factual information on international population issues.** In particular, the following would be desirable:

  — clear explanations of complex demographic concepts, such as "population momentum" (the phenomenon of population growth occurring simultaneously with falling fertility), and their policy implications

  — basic information on population-assistance programs

  — historical information on population-assistance programs, particularly their record on providing culturally appropriate services

  — the relationship between family planning programs and abortion

  — constituent views on population issues.

The respondents indicated that brief (one-page) documents, supported by a longer white paper with a short, highly memorable overview, would be most useful.

ACKNOWLEDGMENTS

The authors wish to thank the congressional staffs who participated in the interviews. The firm of Belden, Russonello, and Stewart conducted the interviews. Partner Kate Stewart, Partner Nancy Belden, and Junior Analyst Jennifer Carkeek were the interviewers.

The authors wish to thank Deborah Hensler and David Chu of RAND for their insightful technical reviews. The helpful comments of Julie DaVanzo, Gar Kaganowich, and Lynn Karoly are also gratefully acknowledged.

Chapter One

INTRODUCTION

This report presents the results of qualitative interviews on population-related issues with legislative directors for members of the U.S. Congress. The interviews were conducted in July and August of 1997.

BACKGROUND AND MOTIVATION

The interviews were conducted for RAND's *Population Matters* project. Unlike most RAND projects, the primary focus of this project is not conducting new research *per se* but rather synthesizing and communicating the findings and implications of existing demographic research in ways that policy audiences and other interested groups will find accessible. The project grew out of the belief, held by many in both research and policy circles, that the results of demographic research are relatively inaccessible to policy audiences and therefore have less impact than they otherwise might.

One of the project's challenges is to identify key policy audiences, understand how research-based demographic information might be useful to them, and devise strategies for communicating it to them effectively. One of these key audiences is the U.S. Congress. Therefore, to help us better understand which areas of demographic research to focus on and how best to convey the findings to Congress, we decided to survey congressional audiences to get a sense of their knowledge and attitudes about population-related issues.

Opinion on this set of issues is highly polarized. Only a relatively small group of members of Congress—a total of 55 identified for our survey (see Chapter 2)—do not consistently vote along ideological lines either for or against population-related measures. As a result, only a few swing votes are likely to determine the outcome of votes on population-related legislation in Congress. It is therefore critical to understand three points about this swing-vote group:

- How they make their choices

- What their attitudes are: For example, is there truth to the commonly held assumptions that current members of Congress tend to be isolationist, desire to cut funding for foreign aid, and regard family planning and other population programs as not valuable?

- How information reaches them and how they use it. In particular, we wanted to obtain a clearer picture of whether and how they make use of research-based information on population issues.

Because the bulk of recent legislative activity has focused on international family planning, and not on other, broader population-related issues, we decided to devote a substantial portion of our qualitative interviews to that subject. We wanted to get a sense of how members of Congress viewed and understood the issue, the relative importance they assigned to it, and whether there were any significant information gaps or strongly held preconceptions that demographic research could usefully address.

We wanted to conduct in-depth interviews and therefore felt there was little chance of directly enlisting members of Congress, who would be highly unlikely to spare 45 to 60 minutes for such a purpose. Instead, we chose legislative directors as a proxy. Legislative directors are the senior policy advisers to members of Congress. They serve on the personal staffs of members and directly advise legislators on specific policy issues. Because of their close working relationships with their employers, legislative directors are in a unique position to know and understand the views of their members of Congress on important issues. Our assumption was that these individuals would have knowledge of the views of their members of Congress on population issues. In answering the questions, the legislative directors indicated that they were speaking on behalf of their members of Congress unless they specifically noted otherwise, which was rare.

ORGANIZATION OF THE REPORT

The remainder of this report is organized as follows: Chapter Two describes our approach and interview methodology. Chapter Three summarizes our results in four areas of discussion: the appropriate role of the United States in global affairs; congressional understanding of specific issues and concepts associated with population policy issues, some of which are under consideration as study topics for the *Population Matters* project; congressional attitudes on issues associated with population growth and international family planning; and the shaping of congressional attitudes and the relative influence of various information sources. Chapter Four draws implications for congressional information needs. The appendix presents the interview questions.

Chapter Two

APPROACH

To collect empirical information, we used an "elite interviewing" approach. Elite interviewing is a qualitative research strategy for gathering information from sophisticated individuals who occupy senior positions (Kempton, Boster, and Hartley, 1957, p. 19; Bernard, 1994). The semistructured format allows the interviewer to tailor the questions to the specific responses and information needs of an individual respondent. It also allows greater freedom for exploring multidimensional topics.

SAMPLE FOR THE STUDY

The universe of desired respondents, which we refer to as the "target sample," was selected based on publicly recorded votes on issues related to foreign relations (usually in connection with appropriations), international family planning, and other population-related issues. We identified members of Congress who were not strongly associated with consistently favoring or opposing initiatives on these issues. This categorization is subjective, based on votes taken in the House and Senate since 1994, when Republicans took over leadership in both houses.[1] However, for members who were in Congress prior to 1994, earlier votes are also taken into consideration. The categorization divided members of Congress into five categories: nearly always support, mostly support, mixed, mostly oppose, and

---

[1]This categorization was developed by an informal consortium of 30 organizations that track population issues on a regular basis.

nearly always oppose. Our sample is drawn from the middle three categories.

The target sample included 44 members of the House and 11 members of the Senate, 24 Democrats and 31 Republicans. Of the 55 legislators in the target sample, 41 had been elected prior to 1994, and 14 came to Congress under the new Republican leadership. Except for their voting records on population assistance and the fact that they were somewhat more likely to have been first elected prior to 1994, our target sample is generally quite similar in characteristics to Congress as a whole (see Table 1).

The assumption underlying this choice was partly that this sample represents the swing vote on population-related policy issues. Given that fact, a striking feature of our target sample is its small size. Approximately 90 percent of Congress consistently votes either uniformly to support or uniformly to oppose population-related legislation. The 10 percent comprising our target sample is thus an extremely critical group because it is likely to determine passage or failure of population-related policy initiatives. Furthermore, we assumed that these members of Congress were less likely to rely on ideologically based information and therefore more likely to have their views shaped by research-based information, to use such information in forming views and reaching policy decisions, and to provide helpful statements about what kinds of information are useful to them.

In all, out of the target sample of 55 legislators, 19 interviews were conducted. Nineteen of the selected offices refused to participate because of office policy not to grant interviews of any nature, and 17 others were never successfully reached (that is, they did not return repeated telephone calls or acknowledge personal visits to their offices).

The interviews were conducted with three Senate and 16 House staff members. Seven legislative directors were from Democratic offices, and 12 were from Republican offices. Table 1 shows the composition of our sample of respondents and how it compares to the target sample and to Congress as a whole. As shown in the table, the respondents slightly overrepresent Republicans relative to the target

Table 1

**Survey Respondents Compared to Target Sample
and to Congress Overall**

	Respondents		Target Sample		Congress	
	Number	%	Number	%	Number	%
Branch of Congress						
Senate	3	16	11	20	100	19
House	16	84	44	80	434	80
Party						
Democrat	7	37	24	44	252	47
Republican	12	63	31	56	282	53
Gender						
Male	18	95	50	91	476	89
Female	1	5	5	9	58	11
Year First Elected						
Prior to 1994	11	58	41	75	355	67
Since 1994	8	42	14	25	179	33
Voting record on foreign relations and population assistance						
Nearly always support	0		0		234	44
Mostly support	6	32	15	27	15	3
Mixed	4	19	13	24	13	2
Mostly oppose	9	47	27	49	27	5
Nearly always oppose	0		0		245	46
TOTAL	19		55		534[a]	

[a]The total does not add to 535, because of a vacancy in the House at the time of the survey.

NOTE: Conservatively, data for the target sample would be statistically significantly different at the 5-percent level from the data for Congress as a whole if the difference exceeded 13 percentage points. Statistics for the sample of respondents would be statistically significantly different from the data for Congress as a whole if the difference exceeded 22 percentage points. A difference between respondents and the target sample is statistically significant if it exceeds 26 percentage points.

sample and to Congress as a whole. Females are underrepresented among respondents (there was only one) relative to the target sample and to Congress as a whole. Respondents were more likely to have been elected since 1994 than the target sample and than Congress as a whole. The distribution of our respondents across the "mostly support," "mostly oppose," and "mixed" (votes) categories is quite similar to that of our target sample. None of the differences just discussed, however, is statistically significant.[2] Hence, our sample of respondents is generally fairly representative of our target sample but overrepresents those elected to Congress since 1994.

INTERVIEW METHODOLOGY

The interviews were conducted in July and August 1997 by senior researchers with Belden, Russonello, and Stewart, an opinion research firm based in Washington, D.C. The list of questions guiding the interviews is presented in the appendix. The respondents were assured that their names and the names of their employers would be held in strictest confidence and that data from the interviews would be aggregated. In most cases, the participating staff members spoke for themselves and their members and identified points on which they differed (this occurred rarely) or on which they were unsure of their employers' opinions. While all the interviews followed the same basic path, each respondent did not address every question listed in the appendix. Some of the staff members anticipated questions and provided answers prior to a question being addressed to them. Others felt they had little to say on a subject, and respondents occasionally cut the interviews short.

The method we used involved semistructured interviews, in which the bulk of the interview is guided by a protocol of written questions asked aloud. In place of a standard questionnaire (in which questions are asked exactly as written and responses are recorded in prespecified categories), these interviews followed a protocol that indicated the general issue areas and specific types of questions that were to be used to gather the information. The questions encouraged paragraph-length rather than word- or sentence-length answers, and the informants were given leeway to elaborate or bring up new topics they considered relevant. In semistructured interviews, probe questions are essential to understand what answers really mean and to explore unfamiliar or unexpected concepts (Bernard, 1994).

---

[2]The small sizes of our respondent and target samples make statistically significant differences unlikely. See the note to Table 1.

After the first ten interviews were completed, the protocol was revised, and the questions were changed slightly to incorporate insights gained during the first phase. The wording of the questions was strengthened to make them clearer to the respondents. For example, terms such as *population momentum* were redefined to make it more apparent why the issue was being raised.

The questions themselves are included in the appendix of this report. Some excerpted quotes from the interviews, which were tape-recorded, are presented in the text. Quotes are identified by the political party of the respondent's employer and their voting record on population issues.

The reader should bear in mind that this research project is highly qualitative, representing in-depth conversations with just 19 staff members. While these data cannot be construed to represent the opinions of all of Congress or of all congressional staff, we do believe they provide insight into the attitudes, knowledge and behavior of the 55 legislators whose records identified them as not completely supporting or opposing population-related programs.

Chapter Three

FINDINGS

This chapter presents detailed results in four areas of discussion: the appropriate role of the United States in global affairs; congressional understanding of specific issues and concepts associated with population policy issues, some of which are under consideration as study topics for the *Population Matters* project; congressional attitudes on issues associated with population growth and international family planning; and the shaping of congressional attitudes and the relative influence of various information sources.

THE ROLE OF THE UNITED STATES IN GLOBAL AFFAIRS

The United States as World Leader

Much has been written in recent years on the question of whether Americans and their leaders are increasingly isolationist (Yankelovich, 1991). Public opinion research has shown that, although Americans believe in helping people in need everywhere, concern for problems at home in the United States, from crime to poverty and education, overshadows Americans' sense of urgency about being active overseas. Likewise, views of the Republican-majority Congress first elected in 1994 suggest that its stance is increasingly indifferent to U.S. overseas involvement and foreign aid in particular.[1]

---

[1]See, for example, Muravchik (1996), pp. 11–12:

> If the spirit of isolationism affected presidential candidates and presidents, it affected Congress even more. While President Bush proposed deep cuts in spending for

The legislative directors we interviewed, however, said their employers believe that leadership from the United States is needed in world affairs. They offered responsibility as a world superpower and the need to protect U.S. interests abroad as the top two reasons the United States needs to remain a world leader. By "U.S. interests," the staff members referred mainly to trade, economic, and environmental interests, as well as national security.

The Role of Aid in U.S. Foreign Policy

Foreign assistance was seen as a useful component of a comprehensive foreign policy. With one exception, all the interviewees said they support foreign assistance. The respondents said their members of Congress believe it is useful in helping advance the U.S. agenda abroad by promoting democracy in developing nations and protecting U.S. economic and diplomatic interests, and it is a worthy humanitarian effort to alleviate suffering in the world.

While foreign assistance was generally viewed as worthwhile for the United States, many legislative directors conditioned their answers by noting that their members of Congress do not consider all aid programs to be equally deserving and that money is sometimes wasted.

While we know that the American public is most apt to offer humanitarian rationales and self-interest as reasons why the United States should be involved overseas,[2] no consistent view of constituent attitudes about U.S. participation in foreign assistance emerged. Of those asked, about half said the constituents of their members of

---

national defense and other international activities, President Clinton proposed deeper ones. But both men found their proposals reduced still further by Congress. The turn away from world affairs by Congress was expressed not only in how it exercised its power of the purse but also in a spirit of indifference. As *Congressional Quarterly* reported in 1993: "As much as Republican presidents used to complain of Congress' 'micromanagement' in foreign policy, today there is the opposite concern—that Congress is not paying close enough attention."

Also see Carroll J. Doherty, "Foreign Policy: Is Congress Still Keeping Watch?" *Congressional Quarterly*, August 21, 1993, p. 2267.

[2]Center for International & Security Studies (1997), Lake Research (1996), Belden and Russonello (1995); *60 Minutes Viewers' Attitudes on Population*, Gordon S. Black Corporation, March 2, 1992.

Congress support foreign aid to some degree, while the other half believe their constituents oppose it.

Acceptance of Global Partnerships

Multilateral partnerships were seen as a strong and desirable approach to foreign policy generally when talking about economic, humanitarian, or environmental concerns. The benefits that the staff members saw deriving from multilateral approaches included sharing the burden for solving problems with other donor countries and the ability of coalitions of nations to be more effective in addressing issues overseas.

However, most cautioned that multilateral partnerships are not always in the best interest of the United States, particularly when national security interests are involved. Some of the drawbacks cited with respect to multilateral partnerships included: concern about the United States getting entangled in alliances counter to our interests; not having an established U.S. policy on an issue; and having reduced influence in decisionmaking.

CONGRESSIONAL VIEWS ON SPECIFIC POPULATION TOPICS

We then asked legislative directors to comment on a series of specific population-related topics and concepts to get a sense of their levels of interest in and understanding of these issues and to identify areas where further research-based information might be useful. Many of the topics were drawn from those under consideration for the *Population Matters* project.

The U.S. Role in Providing International Development Assistance

Overall, the fact that the U.S. spends less money per capita on development assistance than do other nations is not a compelling reason for the United States to give more, according to the congressional staff members. Only a couple of the legislative directors in our study said their members of Congress believed the United States should be trying to provide as much in development assistance per capita as other countries.

Most interviewees rejected comparisons with other countries, saying that, while the United States should contribute at some level, if other countries want to give more per capita than the United States, that is their business. Others argued that comparisons are unfair because other countries have different priorities. For example, a number noted that the United States spends more per capita on defense than do Norway, Japan, and many other countries, which helps provide stability in the world and which is an area of U.S. leadership.

World Population Growth and International Immigration

Only a few respondents associated world population growth with increased levels of international migration. Many respondents believe global migration is a persistent and long-standing problem, regardless of population trends. Some see the main contributors to immigration to be natural disasters and civil strife, rather than sheer population growth.

Many of the respondents believed the United States should be involved in looking for solutions to international migration because the United States ends up with many of the world's immigrants and refugees. The U.S. role here, in the view of these staff members, is to help countries economically and to help them manage natural resources better. The respondents did not link population growth pressures and immigration trends, however, and thus do not see immigration concerns as reason to care about population growth.

Connections Between World Population Growth and U.S. Political Interests

Little, if any connection, was seen between world population growth and U.S. political interests. The legislative directors said their members of Congress believe an expanding world population is not likely to have a political impact on the United States in the foreseeable future.

The Concept of "Unmet Need for Contraception"

"Unmet need for contraception" is a measure of the extent to which women around the world want to limit family size or space births farther apart but do not use contraception. Most of the legislative directors expressed the view that their members of Congress had heard of the concept and accepted the assertion that there is significant unmet need in such places as sub-Saharan Africa. Only a few of the staff members in our study doubted that there is significant unmet need.

Most also believed that increasing health education and the availability of contraceptives—that is, trying to address the unmet need—will in fact lead to lower birth rates.

Some believe, however, that women in developing countries do not want to regulate their fertility and that cultural barriers also stand in the way of decreasing birth rates. For these reasons, they think that just making contraceptives available may be too simple a solution for lowering birth rates.

> It [unmet need] sounds logical but you have to consider the cultural heritage of other countries, and how they feel about birth control. In India, they think any prevention of having children is a bad thing. I think it depends on the geographic area that you are trying to impact. [Republican, mostly support]

This and similar responses suggested that members of Congress would benefit from awareness of the research showing the successful efforts of family planning and related health programs in adapting to local cultural contexts.

The Macrodemographic Issue: Population Momentum

The legislative directors we interviewed were not familiar with population momentum, which is the tendency of a population to continue growing for some time even after women begin having an average of two children each (Population Action International, 1996). When told that demographers project that if women began having just two children on average today, population would still grow from 5.8 billion in 1997 to more than 8 billion before stabilizing in the next century, most of the staff members in our study found the statement plausible. Furthermore, when informed that one of the reasons for this is that the largest teen cohort in history—900 million—is just entering the childbearing ages, most also found that plausible.

Some among the first ten respondents in our study were confused by the concept of population momentum. All who were given a longer explanation, in the second round of interviewing, said they comprehended the concept. However, the explanation of population momentum failed to generate much concern among the legislative directors. While they felt in principle that the momentum explanation described a looming problem, the respondents did not in fact express surprise or heightened concern.

The U.S. Role in Providing International Family Planning Assistance

Most respondents did not know that only 4 percent of U.S. development assistance goes to family planning; upon hearing this figure, over half reported that their members of Congress would consider it too little. A handful thought it was the right amount. No one thought it was too much to spend on family planning programs. One legislative director questioned the accuracy of the figure, and several said they did not feel they were in a position to opine about the adequacy of 4 percent, suggesting the need for further information on funding levels and mechanisms for these programs.

POPULATION GROWTH AND FAMILY PLANNING PROGRAMS

World Population Growth Not a Compelling Problem

Almost all of the respondents expressed that their employers believe world population growth is a problem, but most said it is only *somewhat* of a problem. Only three said it is urgent; these three respondents' members of Congress share certain characteristics: They have been in office a longer time; they are pro-choice; and two of the three are Democrats. The staff of the members of Congress who called population "an urgent problem" did not raise the abortion issue in conversation about funding international family planning. However, those less willing to label it urgent frequently volunteered reservations about funding abortion. The staff of three of the 19 members of Congress saw population growth as a nonissue; all of these members were Republicans with similar voting patterns, labeled "mostly opposed" toward world population issues.

The various reasons world population growth was viewed as an urgent problem included

- threats to U.S. economic interests

- environmental degradation

- strain on limited resources

- increased dislocation of people and immigration

- decreased quality of life for people in developing countries.

While most believed that an increasing world population would eventually affect U.S. economic interests and the environment, they were less certain about threats to U.S. political interests. In addition, few saw an immediate threat to any U.S. interests:

> It is not just that people should not have children, but insofar as you can help prevent runaway population growth that is not intended or wanted, then you are probably doing a service about four generations down the road when the resource depletion and technology have caught up with us. Is it an urgent problem? It is not something that is sitting on top of us at the moment that is threatening anything unless you live in India. It is a long-term problem. [Republican, mixed]

Few believed that U.S. population growth posed problems. One legislative director stated that domestic population pressures would have to be enormous before public policy in the United States would speak about lowering population growth rates in this country.

Interest in International Population Programs

Over half of the staff members said their employers have some or a great deal of interest in programs to address world population growth. The interests of members of Congress stem from a variety of reasons. Some have a particular issue that concerns them, one that is connected to population growth and/or family planning. These include (on the support side) an interest in child survival efforts and improving quality of life around the world, and (on the side of caution) the connection between abortion and population programs. Some admitted their members of Congress have become interested or conversant on the issues chiefly because they were put on a relevant committee. Indeed, others reported that their employers have not cultivated interest in population programs because the members of Congress did not serve on a committee dealing with the issue and/or because there were many other issues that take priority for the representatives and senators.

U.S. Role in Addressing World Population Growth

Many of the interviewees expressed the support of their members of Congress for U.S. leadership on population issues by providing education, technology, resources, and voluntary family planning to developing countries. However, many cautioned that the United States should not dictate to other countries on how to deal with their population problems or become involved in quagmires, such as China's population policy.

Indeed, not all were eager to see the U.S. lead in addressing global population growth. A few of the staff members said the United States should have some involvement, but recommended multilateral approaches, since the United Nations or other international organizations are the appropriate organizations to take the lead on population issues. Two reasons for supporting multilateral organizational leadership on population that the legislative directors offered (in addition to those discussed earlier) were that the United Nations or other multilateral organizations have population programs already in place, and that, by supporting those, the United States avoids situations perceived as imposing its will on other cultures.

Support for Voluntary Family Planning Programs

When discussing family planning specifically, almost all the respondents said their members of Congress supported voluntary international family planning programs. Their stated attitudes on supporting family planning assistance did not vary by party identity, length of time in office, abortion position, or even the mostly support and mostly oppose ratings. The one exception in our interviews was a legislative director in a Democratic office who did not think the United States should be involved in the personal decisions people make about childbearing but that the United States should have a role in addressing world population growth through providing economic assistance.

The congressional staff offered both macrodemographic and micro-level, personal well-being rationales as reasons to support voluntary family planning programs. On the demographic side (addressing population growth), the reasons offered included: lessening the threat of population growth to the world economy, reducing the effects on the environment and natural resources, preventing threats to U.S. national security, and reducing international migration. In terms of personal well-being, legislative directors offered these reasons: promoting the health of mothers and children in developing countries, increasing the quality of life in developing nations, humanitarian reasons, allowing people to make individual choices, and reducing the number of abortions:

> Family planning [is needed] in the sense of educating people, using the technology we have to stop the spread of disease, and using birth control. We don't want to force anything on anybody, but they damn sure should have it available to them. [Republican, mostly oppose]

Awareness of Constituent Opinion

Most respondents said they know how constituents feel about foreign assistance issues and certainly about abortion. Several stated that it depends on the area of the district. Overall, when asked about their constituents, one-half of the legislative directors volunteered that their constituents would favor foreign assistance in general and international family planning specifically; the remaining legislative directors think their constituents would oppose these programs. The legislative directors believe that the constituents who support foreign assistance tend to support family planning efforts, although not necessarily abortion and that the constituents who tend to oppose foreign assistance, also, to a greater extent, oppose family planning programs.

However, the level of active interest by voters in foreign assistance or family planning assistance is low, according to many public opinion surveys (Kull, 1995; Belden and Russonello, 1994), and so we suspect the members of Congress are not overly conscious of voters' views on these matters.

Abortion as a Factor in Tempering Support

The issue of abortion appeared to be fundamental in determining attitudes toward population policies. Contentious and opposing attitudes and beliefs surrounding abortion and the belief or fear that foreign aid for family planning will end up supporting abortions in other countries are driving restrictive policies in the Congress. In the first ten interviews, we did not specifically raise the issue of abortion. However, a number of the respondents whose members of Congress mostly oppose population programs in voting volunteered the possibility that funds would go toward abortion as a reason to oppose foreign assistance for family planning. Those whose members of Congress mostly support population programs were unlikely to raise concern over abortion, mentioning instead their concerns regarding the volume of spending overseas more generally as a possible reason to disfavor family planning assistance.

In the second half of the interviews, we intentionally raised the abortion issue to clarify how the legislative directors and their employers understood arguments for and against restricting family planning funds. We framed this discussion around three votes, called the Paul, Gilman-Pelosi, and Smith amendments to a foreign operations appropriation bill that was pending at the time (September 1997). These amendments proposed to define the uses of foreign aid funding.[3] We set forth these recent amendments to initiate a discussion

---

[3]The so-called Mexico City Policy—a ban on foreign assistance to organizations that perform abortion or provide any information about abortion—was instituted by Executive Order in 1984 by President Reagan and continued during the Bush administration. The prohibition was overturned by President Clinton immediately upon taking office in 1993. Since then, some members of Congress have made efforts to reinstate the policy via legislation placing limits on foreign aid appropriations for international

of how members of Congress make decisions regarding foreign appropriations for international family planning and abortion services.

Supporters of the Gilman-Pelosi effort expressed the view that the abortion issue should not get in the way of fully funded family planning. However, the Gilman-Pelosi effort was defeated, and the more restrictive Smith amendment passed.   Reasons for supporting restrictions centered on a belief that money may be shifted to enable family planning funding to be used for abortion in some way or to permit more abortions if not explicitly prohibited. Furthermore, those who supported restrictions did not believe that restricting family planning services actually increases unwanted pregnancies and therefore also increases abortions. Some did not accept the assertion that more unwanted pregnancies would increase abortion rates. Others were confident that managers of family planning programs would make sure that other options including abortion are made available to women one way or another.

Family Planning Assistance for Americans

Our study also addressed attitudes about public funding for family planning in the United States, to examine whether opposition to family planning within this country has a role in reducing support for services abroad. We found support for the funding of family planning in the United States from about half the offices interviewed, while the others were mainly unsure of the positions of their members of Congress on this issue. General reasons for support of domestic family planning included improving the quality of life and the health of mothers and children. Only one legislative director mentioned reducing population growth as a goal for family planning in this country. Indeed, nearly all the legislative directors rejected

---

family planning. In the 1997 session of Congress, Representative Ron Paul (R-TX) proposed an amendment to the 1998 Foreign Appropriations Act that would have cut off foreign assistance for international family planning, but it was defeated (147 to 278). Representative Chris Smith (R-NJ) proposed another amendment to the same Foreign Appropriations Act to enact a revised version of the Mexico City language that effectively prohibited foreign assistance to any organization that provides abortion services or engages in any activity that would affect its government's policy on abortion.

the notion that the United States has a domestic "population problem."

The main reason to oppose domestic family planning was abortion.
Most of the offices interviewed said they would not support funding
of domestic family planning if the programs included abortion.

ATTITUDE FORMATION AND INFORMATION SOURCES

We talked with staff members about the basis for opinions and policy
recommendations on these issues as well as about information
sources they use in forming opinions and making decisions concern-
ing foreign affairs and specifically about population and family
planning issues. The purpose of this particular line of questioning
was to try to determine the relative role of empirical research in
shaping attitudes and furnishing information in congressional decisionmaking. Knowing about sources of information helps us understand what types of information (for example, advocacy-based or
scientific) people are getting and what additional information may
be needed.

Sources of Influence and Information

Influence of Personal Experiences. Some staff members were able
to identify particular life experiences of the members of Congress
that had shaped their employers' views on foreign affairs, especially
with respect to population concerns. The most commonly named
experience was overseas travel. One staff member also mentioned
the impact of the employer's experience of having served in the
armed forces overseas as contributing to his knowledge of foreign
affairs.

Leaders on Foreign Policy and Global Issues. Congressional staff
referred to many different information sources for information on
foreign affairs, including the appropriate committees, the offices of
other members of Congress, and caucuses.[4]

---

[4]Ben Gilman (R-NY) is offered by many of the House staff as a leader in Congress on
foreign affairs and population issues to whom their members look on these issues.
Also mentioned on the Republican side are Chris Smith (R-NJ), Porter Goss (R-FL),

Sources of Research and Analysis on Population Issues. Legislative directors cited a range of sources for research and analysis on population issues, including the State Department, the U.S. Agency for International Development, United Nations organizations, embassies, advocacy groups, lobbyists, think tanks, newspapers and magazines, and constituent input. On the government side, staff specifically mentioned the U.S. Agency for International Development and the State Department. Among nongovernmental groups, they mentioned Zero Population Growth, the International Planned Parenthood Federation, the National Right to Life Committee, and the Family Resource Council. To date, none had thought of RAND as a source of materials on this issue, but they had a generally high opinion of RAND as a credible source of objective, scientifically based research and analysis.

We also inquired specifically about who approaches the congressional offices to talk about foreign affairs and population issues. The organizations that were listed included Zero Population Growth, InterAction, antihunger groups, the International Planned Parenthood Federation, the National Right to Life Committee, the Alan Guttmacher Institute, the Sierra Club, environmental groups (generically), the Christian Coalition, the U.S. Catholic Conference, the National Family Planning and Reproductive Health Association, the Family Research Council, the American Israeli Public Affairs Committee, and the National Jewish Coalition.

Constituent Input. Attitudes are also influenced by constituent input. To inform members of Congress on these issues, the legislative directors rely on the reports and briefs supplied by interested organizations, as well as concerns and information supplied by constituents. Some offices tend to place more emphasis on constituent input than others, but, for the most part, staff members are looking more to the offices of other members of Congress, think tanks, advocacy groups, and government agencies than to constituents for factual information on population issues.

Amo Houghton (R-NY), Curt Weldon (R-PA), Sonny Callahan (R-AL), Jim Greenwood (R-PA), Mike Bilirakis (R-FL), Dan Burton (R-IN), and Frank Wolf (R-VA). Democrats who were identified as providing leadership on this issue include Howard Berman (D-CA) and Frank Pallone (D-NJ). In the Senate, Republicans Richard Lugar (R-IN) and Jesse Helms (R-NC) were the names mentioned.

Desired Types of Information and Modes of Presentation

Desired Types of Information. The respondents we interviewed suggested that members of Congress would welcome basic information presented in a concise manner. This information included

- Population trend information
- Information on program costs and outcomes:
    - How much money does the United States spend on population programs, and what do the numbers mean?
    - How much U.S. family planning and population money goes to which countries?
    - What are the overall sources of program funding?
    - How do programs spend the money?
    - Who administers the programs?
    - What actually goes on in the programs?
    - How effective are they?
- Program impacts, including an analysis of the potential effects of population growth on U.S. interests and an analysis of the connection between unchecked population growth and U.S. concerns, including environmental impacts, economic impacts, and particularly, national security
- Information regarding American attitudes toward population programs and family planning

Modes of Presentation. Legislative directors cited two modes of presentation as the most influential for members of Congress: short policy briefs and audiovisual presentations, or "briefings." Comprehensive policy papers (30 to 60 pages) were criticized for excessive length, and many legislative directors we interviewed also complained that they receive too many of them.

Policy Briefs or Summaries. Briefs were cited as useful for the "raw" and factual background information they provide. Background papers, short summary documents outlining the key salient issues, were considered particularly useful when they pertain to the work of a committee on which a member sits. The most effective policy briefs are one- to two-page summaries. The National Right to Life Committee, the Alan Guttmacher Institute, and the Heritage Foundation were mentioned as examples of groups that produce this type of summary.

Briefings. Staff briefings are a major mechanism for a member of Congress to receive information on foreign affairs and population issues. The staff members with whom we spoke or others in their offices generally collect and summarize information and then brief the members of Congress on a specific issue, usually when a vote is upcoming. Most of the members of Congress do not read full research reports put out by think tanks or others, except on the occasion that a report pertains to an issue of a committee they sit on, they have a personal interest, or the issue is a very controversial one. Many of the legislative directors reported that members of Congress put a lot of weight on what their staff members say and that staff members play a key role in decisionmaking.

Chapter Four

CONCLUSIONS: IMPLICATIONS FOR CONGRESSIONAL INFORMATION NEEDS

A principal purpose of the interviews with legislative directors was to understand the information needs of members of Congress and their staffs with respect to population issues and to identify any significant information gaps or strongly held preconceptions related to population issues and programs that information based on demographic research could usefully address. We identified several kinds of relevant information:

- **Clear explanations of complex demographic concepts.** Demographic concepts, such as population momentum, are frequently cited by research on international family planning when discussing the record of family planning programs or the continuing need for such programs. Yet congressional staffs did not demonstrate a clear understanding of this concept or its implications for policy.

- **Basic information on population trends and assistance programs.** The legislative directors themselves expressed an interest in seeing descriptive information on population trends, including immigration and population growth, and also on population-assistance programs, including program content, administration, cost, and effectiveness.

- **Historical information on population-assistance programs, particularly their record on providing culturally appropriate services.** We encountered concerns about family planning and other population assistance programs as an imposition of U.S. or Western values on people of other cultures. There is a body of scientific literature dealing with the record of family planning programs in adapting to local contexts.[1]

- **Constituent views on population issues.** The interviews suggested that members of Congress would welcome broader information about constituent opinion and awareness of population issues. Partly in response to this apparent need, the *Population Matters* project is undertaking a nationwide public-opinion survey of population issues.

- **The relationship between family planning programs and abortion.** Family planning and abortion have become inseparably linked in recent congressional debates about U.S. funding of family planning programs, both domestic and international. Some of the congressional staffs seemed unaware that there is a body of research demonstrating that successful family planning lowers the incidence of abortion by reducing unwanted pregnancies. Partly as a result of these interviews, the *Population Matters* project is undertaking a synthesis of research on the relationship between family planning and the incidence of abortion.

_____

[1]This subject is discussed in the *Population Matters* project's first report: *The Value of Family Planning in Developing Countries*, (Bulatao, 1998, p. 35 ff).

QUESTIONS ASKED IN QUALITATIVE INTERVIEWS
WITH LEGISLATIVE DIRECTORS

GLOBAL ENGAGEMENT

1. What do you see (or does your boss see) as the main reasons the U.S. should be a leader in foreign affairs?

2. When thinking about U.S. leadership in the world, should the U.S. have a foreign aid program? IF NOT: Why not?

3. Is foreign aid generally worthwhile to the U.S.? Why?

   In recent years, there has been a multilateral or global partnership approach to dealing with some international issues. In these situations, the U.S. is not always the leader. Is this a good way to deal with these issues, or is the U.S. losing influence by participating in these coalition approaches? What if national security interests are threatened? Does that make a difference in the type of role the U.S. should take?

SCOPE OF THE POPULATION PROBLEM

1. Is world population growth a current problem or has it been resolved? How much of a problem do you feel (does your boss feel) population growth is? Is it an urgent problem? Somewhat of a problem? Why is it a problem?

2. Is world population growth an issue the U.S. should be taking a leadership role in addressing? Why do you think the U.S. should be interested or concerned about world population growth? IF NOT: Who should take the lead? What role should the U.S. play?

3.   How much interest does your member take in the Congressional debates over international population programs: a great deal of interest, only a moderate amount of interest, or a low level of interest? What are some of the reasons for interest or disinterest?

POINTS OF REFERENCE AND SOURCES OF INFORMATION

1.   Who are the leaders your member looks to on foreign policy and global issues within the Senate/House?

2.   Has your member had any specific experiences in life that have greatly influenced his or her thinking on foreign affairs? (Vietnam, World War II, travel, Peace Corps, etc.)

3.   Currently, where does he or she obtain information about foreign affairs? About international programs?

4.   How credible do you find the organizations that lobby you? Are some more credible than others?

5.   What sources of information are used for briefing the member?

6.   What is the relative value of policy briefs (Congressional Research Service, Democratic Study Group, from party leadership or Whip Reports, other internal background papers, external from think tanks, advocacy groups, etc.) as compared to constituency input, advocacy input, other input?

7.   What role do you or other staff have in managing these issues? That is, how do you go about working with the member on this? What role does staff play in decisionmaking? Who else is significant?

8.   Do you generally consider policy research on foreign affairs put out by think tanks to be helpful, or not? Why?

[Question 9 was added in the second set of interviews;]

9.   Which ones are the most helpful, credible? Least? Does your member read research reports? Do you?

10.   What about RAND? What is RAND? Is it a credible group or not?

11. What kinds of research on population programs would be helpful to you?

12. Who normally lobbies your office on the foreign policy and global population issues? Are there some groups that are more credible than others? Why?

CONCEPTS

1. Do you (your member) believe world population growth rates threaten U.S. economic interests? A lot, some, or little?

2. Do you (your member) believe world population growth rates threaten U.S. environmental interests? A lot, some, or little?

3. Do you (your member) believe world population growth rates threaten U.S. political interests? A lot, some, or little?

4. Does the U.S. have a domestic population growth problem? How so? Does legal immigration contribute to it?

5. Is there an international immigration problem? What are its causes (civil strife, economics, natural disasters)? [First set of interviews]

6. How should we deal with international migration? What role should the U.S. play? (Do you see international immigration as part of the population growth problem? Are there national security issues involved in international migration? In what ways? (Drug trafficking? Terrorism?) [First set of interviews]

7. ASK IF RESPONDENT MENTIONS MEXICO: So you consider immigration from Mexico to be a problem separate from other immigration flows? If yes, why? Should it be tackled differently?

8. Let's talk about family planning programs. When thinking about the U.S. role in the world, does your boss believe the U.S. should support voluntary family planning programs overseas? Why? Why not?

9. When it comes to supporting something like the foreign operations appropriation for international family planning funding:

The Paul amendment would have cut all funds for family planning and population control.

The Gilman-Pelosi amendment would have amended the Smith Amendment to allow organizations that use their own funds for abortion to remain eligible for international family planning funding.

The Smith amendment prohibits funding to any organization that "indirectly performs abortions."

The restrictions in the Smith amendment drive the advocates for international family planning crazy because, they say, it ends up limiting the family planning funding available, which drives up unwanted pregnancies and thus abortions. Supporters of the Smith language say the organizations would move money around and fund more abortions. Do you or your member come down on one side or the other on this?

10.   In your (boss's) view, what are the chief reasons to support foreign assistance for family planning?

11.   What are the chief reasons to oppose foreign assistance for family planning?

12.   Should the U.S. fund domestic family planning programs? Why? Why not? What are the reasons for? Reasons against?

13.   Some say there is an unmet need for contraception in developing countries, especially in sub-Saharan Africa, that is, women who want to prevent pregnancy but do not have access to information or medical services to do so. Do you (your boss) think this is true? Do you think the availability of contraceptives would significantly drive down birth rates, or not?

14.   Some say the world is on the verge of another population explosion because 900 million young people, mostly in third world countries, will enter their reproductive years by the year 2000. Have you heard this before? Do you think this is true? If we assume that population explosion is accurate, do you think there is something we should be doing about this?

[Below is part of #14 that was added in the second set of interviews.]

In talking about a population explosion, there is the term *population momentum*. This is the tendency of a population with a high proportion of young people entering child-bearing years, with a smaller proportion of elderly people dying. Demographers project that if women began having just two children on average today population would still grow to 8 billion before stabilizing in the next century. Have you heard this before? Do you think that it is true? Does the population momentum issue make population a more urgent issue?

Returning to foreign aid briefly:

15. Does this ring true: Per capita, the U.S. provides less official development assistance in all areas than most other industrial countries. Have you heard this before? Is this the way it should be?

16. A. The U.S. spends about $0.70 per person per week on foreign development assistance, compared to $1.70 for Japan, and $4.70 for Norway. Is this something you have heard before? Does this comparison matter in your (your member's) view?

    B. Of all U.S. development assistance, 4 percent goes to family planning. Is this something you have heard before? Does this sound like too much, too little, or just about right?

17. Do you think we get stuck having to continue to support programs like family planning once we get them started overseas, or do you think programs like that get taken over by the recipient country, or do you not know about this?

18. What if you learned that about 75 percent of the costs of family planning programs are paid for by the developing countries? Is this something that you have heard before? Does this sound like a good use of foreign assistance, or not?

19. Do you think the people your member represents support foreign assistance?

20. What if it goes for family planning in other countries?

Belden and Russonello, *Pew Global Stewardship Initiative Survey of the American Voters*, Washington, D.C., 1994.

Belden and Russonello, *Understanding American Values,* Washington, D.C., October 1995

Bernard, H. Russell, *Research Methods in Cultural Anthropology*, 2nd ed., Newbury Park, Calif.: Sage Publications, 1994.

Bulatao, Rodolfo A., *The Value of Family Planning in Developing Countries*, Santa Monica, Calif.: RAND, 1998.

Center for International & Security Studies, *The Foreign Policy Gap: How Policymakers Misread the Public.* College Park, Md.: University of Maryland, October 1997

Doherty, Carroll J., "Foreign Policy: Is Congress Still Keeping Watch?" *Congressional Quarterly*, August 21, 1993, p. 2267.

Gordon S. Black Corporation, *60 Minutes Viewers' Attitudes on Population*, Rochester, N.Y., March 2, 1992.

Kempton, William, James S. Boster, and Jennifer A. Hartley, *Environmental Values in American Culture*, Cambridge, Mass.: Massachusetts Institute of Technology, 1995.

Kull, Steven, Program on International Policy Attitudes, Americans and Foreign Aid, March 1, 1995

Lake, Celinda C., and Pat Callbeck Harper, *Public Opinion Polling*, Washington, D.C.: Island Press, 1987.

Lake Research, *Recent Research on Women*, Washington, D.C., 1996.

Muravchik, Joshua, *The Imperative of American Leadership: A Challenge to Neo-Isolationism*, Washington, D.C.: The AEI Press, 1996.

Population Action International, *Why Population Matters*, Washington, D.C.:, 1996.

United Nations Development Program, *Human Development Report 1995*, New York: Oxford University Press, 1995.

Yankelovich, Daniel, *Coming to Public Judgment: Making Democracy Work in a Complex World*. New York: Syracuse University Press, 1991.